When My Son Died...
This Is My Story

When My Son Died...
This Is My Story

A TRUE ACCOUNT OF LIFE, DEATH AND SURVIVAL

Michaline Gregorowicz

When My Son Died...
This Is My Story

ISBN: 978-0-578-21664-5

PRINTED IN USA

In Loving Memory

of

JEFFREY

Contents

Prologue

What do you do when your child dies? It's a scenario none of us ever wants to think about! And we shouldn't! Just scoot the idea right out of your realm of thought. For some believe that sometimes we bring to ourselves what we put out into the universe. Unfortunately, some of us do end up having to face this unspeakable reality. And so on June 12, 2000, I became a member of an exclusive club that no one ever wants to join. For it was on that day that my oldest, handsome, loving and compassionate, twenty-year old son, Joseph died. Needless to say, that one event changed my life forever.

And so eighteen years ago, I began this journey, of living the rest of my life without one of the loves of my life. How would I ever do it? It seemed impossible. I was only forty-eight years old. I remember thinking that I wished I were older, at least 60, so my years without him would not be too many.

So fast forward now to 2018. I have survived for eighteen years, and am now sixty-six years old. But believe me, this so-called journey has not been easy, and it continues to be a struggle, every day without Joseph. It does get easier for sure, but I truly miss him every second of every day.

Over these eighteen years, I have discovered I needed to find ways to work at helping myself continue without him. With the help of my close family and friends, and my own determination, I have been able to do this. Over these years I have also met or heard about other parents who have also lost a child. In some cases, they are doing fine like myself. In other cases, not so much.

Quite a few years ago, I ran into a lovely woman whom we had gotten to know through our sons' sports. Unfortunately, her oldest son had passed away after my Joseph. In addition to him, she also had two other children in their teens. When I started asking her how things were going, I discovered not very well! So I began telling her some of the things I had done that helped me and my family get through Joseph's passing. After about a fifteen-minute conversation, this woman looked at me and said that I had done more to help her in the last fifteen minutes than anyone had done for her since her son died. It was at that moment I decided that I needed to do something to reach out to other grieving families who had also lost a child.

So over the next few years I frequently thought that maybe I should write a book about how I am doing it. If I could just help one parent survive, it would be worth it. But it always seemed like such an incredible undertaking. Every time I would try writing something, I would become overtaken by my emotions and would have to stop. Yet no matter how hard I tried, I could not get this book idea out of my head. So finally, I figured maybe this was my purpose. Maybe I was meant to write this book. So after many years of struggling to do this, here is my story.

Chapter 1

Happiest Day of My Life

*D*ecember 27, 1979, is a day I will never forget. It was the day on which my first son, Joseph, was born. He arrived at approximately 7:30 a.m., after a long labor and delivery. I had been admitted into the hospital around 7:00 p.m. the night before because my water had broken. But none of that mattered. I was now the mother of this beautiful baby boy, blue eyes, 6 pounds 13.5 ounces, 21 inches long. This definitely was the happiest day of my life up to that point. My husband, John, of course wanted to name our baby John. However, since I wasn't sure if we would have any other children, I wanted to pick his name. I guess we both decided on Joseph.

Chapter 2

Saddest Day of My Life

June 12, 2000 is a day I will never forget. It was the day my firstborn son, Joseph, died. He died at approximately 7:30 a.m., after a long night filled with waiting and hoping he would survive. We had rushed him to the hospital the night before. I had stayed with him the entire night in the ICU holding his hand, talking to him, and telling him how much I loved him. But none of that mattered now, because my beautiful son was gone. My husband was now back in the hospital with me, when the nurse came over to tell us that Joey didn't make it. The rest is kind of a blur. John went home to get our younger son, Jeremy, who was fifteen at the time. He also called my sister, Tess, and her family, and my cousin, Denise, and her family, to tell them Joey had passed away.

I remember Jeremy crying at the hospital, asking the nurses to remove all the tubes from Joey, which they eventually did. So with tears flowing from all of us, we all sadly said our goodbyes to Joey. I think I was the last to stay with him. I remember hugging him and kissing him on his forehead, and telling him how much I loved him. But I remember not doing so for too long, because I was afraid I wouldn't be able to let go. And then, we went home without him.

Chapter 3

Welcomed Visitors

So the rest of that Monday on which Joey died included a stream of visitors, his closest friends, their parents, our friends and neighbors. The outpouring of love and support was wonderful. I remember a call from one of Joey's doctors, Dr. Peters. He was so saddened by Joey's passing. He wanted to know what had happened and how we were doing. This wonderful man has also since passed. He was only around 50. Another dear soul gone too soon.

I received a phone call from the girlfriend of the young man whom Joey had been with the day before. She called asking for Joey, knowing, I'm sure, that he had died, but just wanting to have that verified by me.

I called Joey's Kung Fu instructor to let him know about Joey. Joey so loved his Kung Fu and his extended family there. It was one of the things he cherished that gave him purpose in his life.

We also decided on a funeral home in our town for Joey's viewing and funeral. So the funeral director also visited our home that day. Together we made the arrangements and gave him information for Joey's obituary for the newspaper. Looking back at Joey's obituary today, I realize the extent of our sadness on that day. It was short and to the point, so much missing information about Joey's wonderful, brief life.

How this day ended, I don't exactly remember, other than with extreme sadness.

Chapter 4

Planning Joey's Funeral

*I*t was a Tuesday, the day after Joey died. So my husband and I needed to get things done for Joey's viewing and funeral. First of all, we discussed what Joey should wear in his casket. We thought about having him wear his Kung Fu gi, which was the uniform he wore. Again, he so loved his Kung Fu and had tested and received his purple sash that previous February. But upon further discussion, we thought of the times in recent years, when Joey had dressed up in a suit, and how special and grown up that made him feel. So we decided on that. My husband, John, had a nice black suit coat which would fit Joey. The rest, a white shirt and black pants, we shopped for that day.

We stopped at our local florist who knew Joey and us through little league, and picked out flowers. Then we went with the funeral director to pick out Joey's casket and finalize arrangements.

We bought three plots at the cemetery where my mom and dad are buried. One for Joey, one for John and one for me. I remember we discussed that my younger son Jeremy, would probably get married someday and would be buried next to his wife. So we wouldn't need a plot for him.

Lastly, we made arrangements at our church for his funeral. My wonderful cousin, Jay, picked out and would deliver the readings for the funeral Mass. We picked out the music and pall bearers, all who were Joey's good friends.

Back in 2000, the "new practice" was to make a collage of photos of your deceased loved one. No videos back then. So later that day, we dragged out the boxes of photos from the last twenty years, which I never had time to put into albums. Then we started going through them. John, Jeremy and I sadly spent hours going through all these wonderful memories of our family. One by one, we picked photos of Joey, which we felt would tell the story of what a loving and happy person he had been, and how many wonderful memories we had all made with him in those short twenty years.

Chapter 5

Joey's Viewing

The day of Joey's viewing was a Wednesday. The viewing hours were two to four p.m. and seven to nine p.m. My wonderful friend Jane volunteered to stay at our house that day while we were gone, because the newspaper had printed our home address in Joey's obituary. We decided it would be a good idea not to leave our house unattended.

So the times we were at the funeral home, Jane was at our house. Thank goodness she was, because the outpouring of love and support from our family and friends was amazing! Jane was there for all the deliveries of gifts of food and drinks. It was phenomenal and so appreciated, because the last thing on our minds that day was what will we eat or drink today. It also enabled us to feed all our wonderful family and friends who visited with us between and after viewing hours.

My memories of Joey's viewing are patchy. I remember John and Jeremy and I were of course the first to see him. I remember thinking how handsome Joey was and how proud he would be getting all dressed up.

I remember not crying too much. I am a very strong person who can somehow always pull it together when I have to.

I remember my son Jeremy sitting in a corner of the funeral home with his friends. He had a baseball cap on and looked so sad.

I remember a group of my coworkers and supervisors, making the seventy-mile roundtrip journey from our office to come to Joey's viewing. Two in particular were crying their eyes out. I remember comforting them and saying it would be alright.

I remember Joey's instructor and friends from the Kung Fu Academy coming dressed in their Kung Fu gis. His instructor gave a little speech and they did a little ceremony for Joey. I remember thinking how happy they probably made Joey that day.

I remember Joey's friend, Jake, whom Joey had been with the night before he died, coming to the viewing. He looked so distraught! He hesitated coming near Joey's casket. I remember going to him and giving him a big hug, trying to comfort him.

The rest is a blur! There was a constant flow of family, friends and acquaintances giving us their condolences. Lots of hugs, kisses and tears that day!

Between the viewing hours, a lot of family and friends visited with us at our house. I remember thinking that I didn't want to deal with all of that. So for some of those interim hours, I laid on our living room couch pretending to sleep, even though I never dozed a second. I remember listening to all the conversations going on in the other rooms. It was my escape, if only for a little while.

After the viewing hours, family and friends again came back to our house. I remember our close friends from the Lehigh Valley, where we had lived for fifteen years, being there.

I remember sitting in our living room with Joey's friends and reminiscing about the good times. How wonderful that was! I can't imagine that Joey's friends realized what a godsend they were for me that night.

After all our company left our home that night, and John and Jeremy went to bed, I sat alone in our living room thinking about Joey. I guess I was thinking about his funeral the next day. All the arrangements had been made, readings and music chosen. But I kept thinking that I somehow wanted to honor Joey more. Then it hit me, his eulogy! We hadn't prepared for that. Our pastor would give the generic eulogy, which would certainly be nice. However, he didn't really know Joey well. Then it occurred to me, who better to write Joey's eulogy than someone who knew him the best, me, his mom. So I grabbed some paper and a red pen and started to write. It came so easily because I wrote from my heart. After scratching out the original, I rewrote it so it would be legible, so someone else could read it if necessary. I was happy because this is how I could honor him!

Chapter 6

Joey's Funeral

I honestly don't remember much of that day. It was a Thursday. I do remember after all our family and friends paid their final goodbyes to Joey at the funeral home, and were all lined up to head over to our church, John, Jeremy and I paid our final respects. Normally at that point, we would have covered Joey up with the blanket before they closed the casket. But earlier Joey's friends, most of whom were pallbearers, offered to do that for us. I think, not only did they help us out, but also themselves. It gave them a chance to say their goodbyes to their good friend, Joey.

Next came the funeral mass. My memories are few. The church was pretty full. We had told our pastor that I would give the eulogy. That would happen after everyone received Holy Communion. After I received, I went down to the basement to use the restroom, because I knew I would have a long time to go until after the service at the cemetery. I remember thinking that if I made a quick beeline to the restroom right after I received Communion, I would have more than enough time to get back to my seat before Joey's eulogy. But as I came back upstairs and walked to my seat in the front of the church, everyone was just sitting quietly. As I sat down, John told me it was time for the eulogy.

I walked up to the pulpit with Joey's eulogy in my hands. I remember looking at all the people. In particular, my eyes landed on two mothers of Joey's best friends. There were tears in their eyes and they were holding onto each other for dear life. I could feel the tears welling up in my eyes. I realized at that point, that the only way I would get through it, was to not look up at anyone, and just read Joey's eulogy.

And so I did, and it went beautifully. My heart was happy. I had given the proper sendoff to my wonderful son, Joey, one of the loves of my life.

The rest is a blur. I don't remember anything about the service at the cemetery. The next thing I remember is the luncheon afterwards. We had it at the restaurant where my younger son, Jeremy, worked. It was filled to capacity with family and friends.

Afterwards, we all returned to our home. I remember standing at our front living room window, watching all of Joey's friends, who had been so devoted for the last few days, say goodbye to each other and then, one by one, they drove away. I remember thinking that now, for the most part, they would return to their lives. But for us, our lives without Joey were just beginning.

Chapter 7

The Nightmare Continues

The days, then weeks, after Joey died were indescribable. Personally, I just ached all over. Getting up in the morning, taking a shower and just making it through the day, were major accomplishments for me.

John had returned to work soon after Joey died, since he worked as a salesman mainly out of his office in our house. I was home from work on medical leave, which would eventually last approximately five months. Jeremy was on summer vacation from school. He had just finished ninth grade.

While John and Jeremy with heavy hearts, tried to resume their normal lives, mine was temporarily put on hold. I was left to deal with the aftermath of Joey's death. This is the part that no one really thinks about, but someone has to do it. Because Joey had been hospitalized the night before he died, the insurance statements, and hospital and doctor bills started arriving. And as we all know way too well, none of this ever goes smoothly. I remember every morning, psyching myself up, to make as many phone calls as I could manage, in order to resolve the issues. The main problem was trying to get through these calls without breaking down into tears, which happened a lot. I actually felt sorry for the people on the other end of the phone. Suddenly, I was this blubbering idiot, trying to explain that my son was covered by medical insurance, but was no longer responsible for anything else because he had died. Eventually after weeks of calls, all of these issues were resolved.

The next task that I found myself responsible for, was sending out thank you notes for all the money, flowers, food and whatnot that our family and friends had been so generous with giving us. These days after a funeral, many families send a generic pre-typed thank you with their family's signature. Some even put a thank you note in the local newspaper. I completely understand this! But back when Joey passed, the norm was a handwritten thank you. I was so totally grateful for all the kindness that was bestowed on us, that I tearfully and painstakingly handwrote a detailed personal note to all. I thanked them for each specific gift they had given us. It probably took me about two months to finish. But in hindsight, I think it was a blessing, because for those toughest months after Joey died, knowing I had to write these thank you notes gave me a reason to get up every morning. It gave me purpose and helped take my mind off of the fact that afterwards, life would have to continue without Joey.

Chapter 8

The Healing Begins

*A*fter *my dad passed away in November of 1985, I remembered* thinking to myself, how would I survive without him? It seemed impossible! Then I thought, I have two choices, I could live or I could die. Well certainly dying was never an option. I had two little boys, Joey was five and Jeremy only around seven months. I knew they needed their mom. So somehow, I managed to find ways to continue my life without my dad.

So here I was again, fifteen years later, faced with a similar dilemma. How could I survive without Joey? But this was much worse! Of course, I loved my dad, but this was my son! It seemed insurmountable. But I knew I had to try and be strong, especially for Jeremy. I knew he still needed me. So my journey without Joey would begin.

Chapter 9

Photographs

*A*s we had gone through twenty years of photographs getting prepared for Joey's viewing, I remembered feeling so wonderful for at least a few moments, seeing all the special times we had shared with Joey. So this is where I would begin. Another special project for myself to help me survive.

I decided to create little themed photo albums, based on the photos we had chosen, Baptism, birthdays, holidays, Cub Scouts, sports and so on, of both Joey and Jeremy. I even got together a small album for Jeremy, which included moments he and Joey had shared together. Unfortunately, some moments you take for granted until it's too late. One special set of photos, which still sticks out in my mind, was of Joey helping Jeremy learn to ride a two wheeled bike.

Back when we lived in the Lehigh Valley, the first two wheeled bike we bought for Joey was his "Knight Rider" bike. That was one of Joey's favorite television shows, "Knight Rider," at the time. The two main characters of the show were "Michael Knight" and his car "Kitt." Not only could "Kitt" speak but was pretty much indestructible. Together "Michael" and "Kitt" fought crime and caught the bad guys.

[1] Joey and all his little buddies loved this show. So for either Christmas or his birthday, which was also in December, we bought Joey his "Knight Rider" bike. It was a twelve or thirteen inch black two wheeled bike with training wheels. It had "Knight Rider" stickers all over it.

Not only did Joey love it, but with it being so small and low to the ground, it was the perfect bike to learn on. Joey barely used the training wheels, and was riding the bike by himself probably by the time he was five. Moving up to a twenty-inch bike later was easy.

So we saved the bike. When Jeremy was ready for a two wheeled bike, he inherited Joey's "Knight Rider" bike. And true to form, on that magical day in May, with Joey's assistance, Jeremy, slow but sure, started riding the bike by himself with no training wheels. He was probably no more than three. I remember it was May, because it was the day before Joey was to receive his First Holy Communion. It had to be through the guidance of angels that I had a camera in my hand, and was able to capture this momentous event. The result was a series of still shots, starting with Joey holding the back of the bike, and ending with Joey letting go, and Jeremy cruising alone. I had truly forgotten about those photos. Little did we know at the time, what a treasure we would have and cherish for so many different life-changing reasons. One thing was obvious in all the photos of Joey and Jeremy together though, and that is how much Joey loved Jeremy. You can see it in his eyes and the way he looked at Jeremy in those photos. That love, that special bond that two brothers share, will never die.

More Photographs

When I realized how much peace photos of Joey gave me, I decided they might help his friends as well. So I picked out a few special photos of Joey: his senior photo, the day he tested and earned his purple Kung Fu sash, and one of him playing John's guitar in our garage. I proceeded to have some five by seven copies made for myself and some wallet sizes made for family and friends. Remember, eighteen years ago, you didn't go to the drug store with a camera card to just print photos, or download them to your computer and send them somewhere to print. They had to be sent out for copying. So this process took weeks. But the result was amazing and I had wonderful memories of the happy, special times in Joey's life to share with family and friends.

Chapter 10

Walking

I had been a pretty avid walker for about three years when Joey passed away. Anytime I was feeling down or tired, or needed to think something through, I found that walking helped me. I guess our body produces good chemicals like endorphins when we exercise, that actually do help us feel better. Since I now had all the time in the world, I decided walking couldn't hurt. Since it was summer, it was a great time of year to start again.

So I walked as much as I could. As I did, I discovered many beautiful things. There are two parks in our area that are connected by a walking bridge that goes over the river. Both parks have walking trails. One park includes playgrounds, baseball and soccer fields, and partly goes along the river. The other park and its trails go through woods, around baseball and football fields, past playgrounds and also partly along the river.

So as I started walking almost daily through these parks, I began to notice things that before I had always been too rushed to notice. I noticed the ducks swimming in the river, the large blue crane flying above the river, and sometimes even fishermen and kayakers paddling down the river. As I ventured on the path through the woods, I noticed squirrels scampering up trees, the rabbits scurrying past me, and even a few deer here and there. As I looked around me, I began to notice the wonders of nature in the trees, bushes and plants. What beauty, what colors, what smells! I eventually would experience the seasonal changes in the scenery around me, as I would continue to walk through the following spring and even longer. It was always a healing experience.

Chapter 11

Photography

*A*fter having discovered how much the photos of Joey had helped me through these tough times, I decided taking more photos might continue to help me through the even tougher times ahead. I had a wonderful little Kodak camera which took great photos. And so I began.

My first photos were of nature. I took many pictures of the beauty I found in the two parks, where I walked, that I mentioned earlier. The results were amazing photographs covering all four seasons. There were photos of trees, bushes, flowers, animals, butterflies, the river, the walking bridge, and anything else I found to be interesting. I eventually put together a few photo albums for each park. I still, to this day, enjoy looking at these albums, and remembering the peace this venture brought to me.

Since my younger son Jeremy was very much into sports, baseball and football specifically, I found him to be a perfect subject for my new-found hobby as well.

So for the next three years, you would find me on the sidelines of Jeremy's games, snapping photos of him and his teammates, hopefully making some memories we would eventually look back on with smiles.

Chapter 12

Tie Dying and Other Stuff

Tie Dying

*P*robably *about a year or so after Joey passed, I became kind of* obsessed with tie dying. Again, not sure why. I had been in high school and college during the mid to late sixties and early seventies when it was a fad, so maybe it reminded me of those more carefree years of my life. So I tie dyed clothing for almost everyone, John, Jeremy, my niece Katie, my cousin Denise's daughter Carla, and my friend Sabrina's son and daughter. I tie dyed shirts, sweatshirts and scarves. It was great! All of the recipients of my tie-dyed creations were so kind. Whether they liked the items I gave them or not, they graciously accepted and wore them. They certainly gave to me when I needed it most, more than I ever could've given to them.

Most recently I've been noticing a resurgence of tie-dyed clothing. Look out family and friends!

Angels and Betty Boop

I don't consider myself to be a very materialistic person, and I do realize having a lot of stuff doesn't necessarily make you happy. However, there is that "special stuff" that can brighten your day.

In my lifetime, I don't really remember having a lot of collections, even as a child. But sometime before Joey died, for whatever reason, I started collecting angels. As I recall, it was a modest collection. But after Joey died, the angel gifts began coming. I received beautiful angel figurines from family and friends, to the point that I now have a curio cabinet filled with these treasures!

Another guilty pleasure which also began before Joey passed was my fascination with the cartoon character Betty Boop.[2] Not sure how it started. I did love this cartoon character as a child, and did remember watching her cartoons on television. Maybe somehow, she also sparked memories of happy, carefree times. But again, after Joey died, many wonderful family members and friends gifted me beautiful Betty Boop figurines, clothing, DVDs, purses and more! The great thing about many of the Betty Boop items is that they have bling! So in addition to all the amazing Betty Boop items I can wear and use in my everyday life, I also have another curio cabinet filled with Betty Boop figurines and more. It may sound crazy, but on any day, but especially on a sad day, a little Betty Boop sparkle goes a long way!

So on days when I need an emotional pick me up, I'll just stand and admire, and sometimes hold in my hands, the beautiful angels and Betty Boop figurines that people have given me over the years. To me these are not just things. Rather they represent the love and caring of family and friends that I have been blessed with over the years. They will always be special and will always bring me joy.

Chapter 13

Sunday Breakfasts

A *little tradition we started after Joey passed was my husband John* and I, getting together with my sister Tess and brother-in-law Sam, my cousin Denise and her husband Paul, and sometimes our kids, for restaurant breakfast on Sunday mornings. I think I'm the only one who considered this a tradition, but it was something that I would look forward to at the end of each week. Getting together with my family and a lovely breakfast, somehow helped with dealing with the loss of Joey. I think it helped because for at least one morning a week, I would get together with people I knew not only loved me and Joey, but on their own level, were going through their own living without Joey too. As a forever close-knit family, we were all helping each other through our grieving process.

This Sunday ritual would continue for about ten years. We don't get together for Sunday breakfasts very much these days. The kids have grown up and our lives have changed. My sister and brother-in-law now split their lives between being snowbirds in Florida through the winter, and living with their daughter and son-in-law during the summer months in Pennsylvania. My cousin and her husband have responsibilities that fill up their Sunday mornings. John and I still go for breakfast on most Sundays. It actually still is special for me, giving me something to look forward to and making me happy. But for all those years after Joey died, our Sunday morning breakfast was a tradition which was part of my salvation. I will be eternally grateful to all of them, for making time for John and I at least one day a week, during a time I consider to be our darkest hours.

Chapter 14

Emma

here do I begin to tell you my story about Emma? When Joey was about fifteen years old, he got a part-time job working at a local fast food restaurant. Also working there was a young woman named Emma. She was about a year older than Joey. They became friends and their friendship grew into love. This girlfriend/boyfriend relationship would last for about two years. It would end when Joey was about seventeen. But even after they parted as girlfriend and boyfriend, they would remain close friends for the rest of Joey's life.

After their romantic relationship ended, I rarely saw Emma, although Joey stayed in touch with her. As I would learn later, Joey would phone Emma often to talk, many times in the wee morning hours. Sadly, the next time I would see Emma would be at Joey's viewing.

About a month or two after Joey died, I received a surprise phone call from Emma. This was to be a phone call that would change my life in a wonderful way. Emma wanted to know if we could get together for a visit. I was so happy to hear from her, so we planned a visit at my house.

It was so nice to see Emma. Being with her brought back memories of happy times in Joey's life. As we visited, she said she had a dream that she wanted to share with me. In her dream, Joey called her on the phone. She could see him on the phone talking to her. He was on one side of the room, she on the other. She said it was a big room, like a banquet hall. He said to her, "Call my mom." So lucky for me, she did as Joey asked and called me. From that day until the present, we have become dear friends. I know Joey purposely brought us together. And I thank him every day for bringing Emma back into my life.

Emma would have dreams of Joey, probably for about the next six months to a year. She would share these dreams with me. She said they were lovely dreams in which she and Joey basically spent time together talking. For example, in one dream she and Joey were sitting on her front porch just talking. But she said, the funny thing was, that when she would wake up after these dreams, she would feel like she had actually been with Joey. She said they were so real!

When I told one of my friends, Sabrina, about Emma's dreams, she told me that the reason these dreams about Joey seemed so real was because they probably were. She said the dreams about Joey were probably visits from Joey. She shared that sometimes when people pass, in order to talk to loved ones they have left behind, they visit them when they sleep. The reason is when we sleep, we are open to such visits.

I will discuss my friend Sabrina in further detail later on. But the point of this story about Emma is that to this day we are still wonderful friends, even though we may not see each other for months at a time. She has since married a wonderful man. They have three amazing daughters. So I also have the honor of spending time with her beautiful family. I am grateful for Emma and her friendship.

So as you go through your grieving process, don't be afraid to develop new friendships. There may be an Emma in your life who will be a part of your salvation, and a child who may bring you both together without you even asking.

Chapter 15

Pearl Jam

I will never forget this one special night, when I was walking up our stairs to get ready for bed. It was probably in the spring, because it was just a few months before Joey died that June. As I headed for my bedroom at the top of the stairs, Joey came almost running out of his bedroom to grab me. "Mom, come here. You have to listen to this Pearl Jam[3] song!" Well, I didn't have a clue who Pearl Jam was, but as I listened to the song, I told Joey that I had heard it before and liked it. So then he proceeded to go down a list of about five reasons as to why Pearl Jam was such a great band, and why they would endure. As I tried to repeatedly retreat to my bedroom to get ready for bed, Joey kept saying, "just one more song, Mom, just one more song." So I did listen to a few more but finally did go to bed. Needless to say, I wish I had stayed up all night, and listened to Pearl Jam songs with Joey. But I will always cherish the memory of that night, and thank Joey every day for introducing me to the band Pearl Jam.

Not long after that, Joey approached me to ask if I would purchase tickets for him and his friends to see Pearl Jam in concert in a park in Albany, New York. I think it may have been that August. He told me he would die if he didn't see them. So I told him I would gladly purchase tickets. Rarely did Joey have such enthusiasm for something. He sounded so happy! So I think I purchased about six or eight tickets. The cost was pretty minimal. Joey told me his friends would reimburse me, but I really didn't care.

Unfortunately, Joey didn't make it to that concert. But his friends did. They wanted my son Jeremy to join them, but since he was only fifteen, we were skeptical about him going with a bunch of twenty-year olds. I'm sure they would've certainly taken care of him, but we decided against it. Since that time though, John, myself and Jeremy have each seen Pearl Jam in concert a few times.

My one regret about that concert, was that Joey never got to see them live. But my cousin Denise put it best when she said that I shouldn't feel too bad, because Joey probably had the best seat in the house!

So because of Joey's love of Pearl Jam's music, John, Jeremy, myself, and many of Joey's and Jeremy's friends have become fans.

So listen to the music! It may be your deceased loved one reaching out to you. When I hear the Pearl Jam song "Corduroy," I picture Joey standing in his bedroom, playing it on his purple Stratocaster. Or when I hear their song, "Low Light," I see Joey sitting in the front passenger seat of my car, strumming his air guitar to it. Sometimes when I'm down and out, one of my favorite Pearl Jam songs will play on the radio and cheer me up. All I can do is smile and say, "Thank you, Joey."

Chapter 16

The Evolution of Joey's Cemetery Stone

The Cross

*A*fter *Joey passed away, we knew it would probably be a while before* we could afford to buy a stone for his grave. But we knew we could probably figure out a way to put a nice, reasonably priced marker there temporarily. So we asked my cousin's husband, Paul, who is a carpenter by trade, if he would make a wooden cross. And so he did. A very nice one, which we still have to this day. Can't bear to part with it.

So our next task was to somehow put Joey's name on the cross. I decided that stenciling might work. So I bought some stencils and purple paint, since Joey had earned his purple sash in Kung Fu before he passed. I stenciled his name in purple letters and it came out beautifully. But still something was missing. Then it came to me. I would stencil a picture of Joey's purple Stratocaster guitar on the cross also. So I took a few photos of his guitar, and made a stencil. It came out great! My husband varnished the finished cross and we placed it on Joey's grave. It was an awesome tribute to Joey for about two years, until we were able to afford to buy a granite engraved stone.

I think at this point, it would be worth sharing, why we chose to put a picture of Joey's guitar on his cross.

Sometime before Joey's birthday in 1999, which is December twenty-seventh, John decided he wanted to buy a guitar for Joey. It would be his birthday and Christmas present since it would be an expensive gift. Joey had wanted a new guitar for some time. So one day, John, a lifelong guitar player himself, and Joey, set out on their mission to buy a guitar. I was not with them, so I'll retell the story the best I can. Supposedly, they went to a few music stores and found this beautiful "purple" electric Stratocaster guitar. Joey fell in love with it! However, it was a little pricey, so they continued to look. But the more John thought about it he said, "What the heck! Why buy something Joey had to settle for. I might as well buy him what he truly wants." John said that Joey's eyes lit up! It was the last major birthday gift Joey would ever receive from us, and the last birthday he would celebrate with us on earth. It was his twentieth birthday.

Thank God John chose to buy it for him. Joey played and enjoyed that guitar until the day he died. Many times, John, Joey and John's cousin would spend a Sunday afternoon jamming and playing the blues. Or many times Joey would just jam alone in his bedroom, playing a Pearl Jam or Stevie Ray Vaughn[4] song. Joey truly enjoyed playing that purple Stratocaster until the day he died.

Our younger son Jeremy inherited the Stratocaster. He never played or showed an interest in playing guitar. Needless to say, after Joey died, he became a self-taught guitar player. He may only occasionally play, but he enjoys Joey's guitar to this day. Since then, he has also acquired a few acoustic guitars. But I am sure that every time Jeremy enjoys playing Joey's Stratocaster, he is looking down on him with a huge smile on his face.

The Stone

I would say approximately a year after Joey died, John and I decided to go on a weekend bus trip to Atlantic City, New Jersey. A few other couples we knew were also going. The only thought that kept coming into my mind was that maybe I would get lucky and win enough money to buy a stone for Joey's grave. It had barely been a year since he passed and the sadness was still quite unbearable.

I remember it was a Saturday as we walked down the boardwalk to the Tropicana Casino. We went up the escalator. When we got to the top, I noticed there were "Wheel of Fortune[5]" slot machines to the right. So I hustled over to them and sat down at an available machine on the end of the row. I put a twenty-dollar bill in and began to play. Only a few hits later, I landed on "Spin." So before I hit the button to spin, I remember thinking, "come on, Joey, let me win something so I can buy you a cemetery stone." I pushed the button and looked up to see where the wheel would stop. Lo and behold, it stopped on one thousand credits. Thinking I was on a twenty-five-cent credit machine, I was thrilled that I won two hundred and fifty dollars. Then the person next to me says, "Congratulations, you won a thousand dollars!" Little did I realize that I was on a dollar credit machine. I did in fact win one thousand dollars! For the rest of that afternoon I couldn't seem to lose and ended up winning about fifteen hundred dollars. This was a nice amount for buying Joey's stone.

So the following May, a month or so shy of the second anniversary of Joey's death, a beautiful black granite monument was placed on his grave. We picked black because we felt that's what he would've picked himself. We also had one of his senior high school photos engraved on the stone. Until this day, I will never forget my little wish to Joey in my mind. Coincidence? You be the judge.

Chapter 17

"Compassionate Friends"

A few weeks after Joey died, John ran into someone who knew about Joey. This person told John about a support group called "Compassionate Friends." This group is composed of parents whose children have died. There was a chapter that held their meetings one evening a month, at a location close to us. So soon after, John attended a meeting. He said it helped him and felt it might help me. I wasn't ready to try for a few months, but eventually I went to a meeting. The group was phenomenal! I pretty much did nothing but sob for the first few meetings. But everyone was wonderful and they all understood, because they too had all been there. Eventually the crying stopped, and I was able to start participating. It was great because you got to talk with and share your feelings with people who knew exactly what you were going through, because each of them was going through it also. On your deceased child's birthday, you could bring in their photo and a birthday cake, and everyone would join with you to celebrate their life. In addition to the monthly meetings, we had potluck dinners, balloon send-offs and other events in memory of our children. Other family members and friends could attend. My sister Tess and my brother-in-law Sam often did. They were always so supportive in remembering their nephew.

One of the traditions of "Compassionate Friends" which I love the most is putting up a Christmas tree in one of our local malls. Anyone who has lost a child, sibling, grandchild, whether they belong to the group or not, can put an ornament with their loved one's photo and/or name on the tree. On the first Sunday in December the tree goes up, and a tree lighting ceremony around the tree follows, in honor of our children. Just thinking about it makes me tear up, but in a good way.

We attended the monthly meetings for about two years, when other responsibilities prevented us from going. But I will be eternally grateful to the people in that group who helped John and me so very much. And until this day, every Christmas season, the ornaments we made with Joey's photo on them, are still on the "Compassionate Friends" tree. And every year, as we Christmas shop, we always visit and spend some moments at the tree. Although it is still sad for us, it is also comforting to know that many people including our family and Joey's friends, still visit the tree and remember him. I recommend, without hesitation, this wonderful group or a similar one, to anyone who has lost a child.

Chapter 18

Seek Professional Help

Very soon after Joey died, I knew in my heart I would seek professional help to get me through these darkest of days. Fortunately, Joey had been seeing Dr. Peters whom I spoke of earlier. He was a psychiatrist. So first chance I got, I made an appointment with him, which as I recall wasn't until August, at least two months after Joey died.

I remember my first appointment. I pretty much sobbed through the entire thing. Dr. Peters was so understanding. He did prescribe medication for me, including something to help me sleep. I would continue to see him monthly, as long as I was taking medication.

He also set me up with one of his psychologists, Darla. I would continue to see her for a year. She was so caring and helpful, especially during the first few months. We would talk and she would send me home with worksheets to complete for our next appointment. I remember just trying to fill out these worksheets was sometimes too overwhelming. But I would do the best I could. Darla was always so caring, sweet and compassionate. I will always be thankful for all the help she gave me.

One thing I do remember Darla telling me is that there are a certain number of steps in the grieving process, and that we need to go through these steps if we hope to heal. We may think we can skip a step, but we can't. If we do, we will eventually have to come back and go through it. Some people think this theory is a bunch of bull, but I don't. I truly believe we all need to go through a grieving process. I think it will take us longer to heal or not to heal at all if we don't. I saw it with my loved ones around me. It just makes sense to me.

So some think there are five, seven or even more steps in the grieving process. I don't remember how many steps Darla gave me to try to work through, but here are some of the points I do remember.[6]

Probably the first step is that you don't want to believe it. You are in denial because the truth is so painful. Eventually the reality of the situation kicks in.

Anger is definitely a natural part of the grieving process. The pain of losing your loved one turns into anger. You are angry at them for leaving you. You resent them for doing things that you feel led to their death. You get angry with other family members or friends. This is all normal. In your heart you know that none of them are to blame. However, you're feeling bitter because you are in unspeakable pain. Sometimes this anger makes you feel guilty, and then you feel angry again. It's like you're on an emotional roller coaster.

Another step in the grieving process is what I like to call the "what ifs." What if I had called him earlier? What if I had taken him to the hospital? Again, this is normal because we feel powerless, so unable to control the situation. I still find myself eighteen years later saying what if this or that. But I stop myself quickly because it really doesn't matter.

Depression is also a step in the grieving process. When your loved one dies you are beyond sad. At first you worry about practical things like the funeral or going back to work. Later this extreme sadness turns more personal. You realize you have to figure out how to continue your life without them. In both cases, with the love and support of family and friends, and sometimes with professional help, you get through this depression.

Probably the most difficult stage of grieving is finally accepting the death of a loved one and making peace with it. Not everyone achieves this. The circumstances surrounding a loved one's death are all different and sometimes make acceptance unattainable. Maybe they died tragically or were very young. Whatever the reason, acceptance never happens.

I realize this is a very simplified explanation of the grieving process. The important idea to remember is that coping with the death of a loved one is very personal. Everyone grieves differently and at their own pace. There is no deadline for the grieving process. Also what works for you may not work for others. No one can understand what you are going through. However, others may be able to console you through your grieving. Allow them to do this. Also allow yourself to be sad, to cry. Yell or scream if you have to. Resisting such emotions will only prolong your grieving process.

Chapter 19

Christmas Without Joey

*B*oth Joey and my younger son Jeremy loved the holidays, especially Christmas. After my mom passed away in 1992, I picked up the torch and started the new tradition of having our Christmas day celebration at our house. And it was always such a nice get together. We would break out the good dishes and celebrate our feast in our dining room. Wonderful memories were made every year.

So how could we possibly go on in 2000, having this Christmas without Joey. I truly didn't know if I would be able to do it. But since Jeremy was only fifteen years old, I knew I had to do it for him.

Then one day my cousin Denise said, "Why don't you do a special tree in Joey's memory." To my cousin I will be eternally grateful. So that is where we started.

So after much thought and discussion with my family, we came up with the colors we would use on our Christmas tree. Since green was Joey's favorite color, we decided to do some green. The rest would be purple because it seemed to be a significant color for Joey. This year, the last Kung Fu sash

Joey tested for and earned was purple. John had bought Joey his purple Stratocaster guitar for his twentieth and last birthday, which Joey personally chose and loved. Lastly, it was the color purple we had used on the wooden cross we placed on Joey's grave. So purple and green it would be.

The first Joey tree was simple. I bought green and purple ribbon, and made simple bows for the tree. I found this lovely shiny purple garland with cut out shapes of little purple angels attached. Lastly, I found lights the closest to purple I could get. They were more magenta, but they were beautiful. And so we created our first Christmas tree in memory of Joey.

Over the years, the tree has evolved beautifully. The magenta lights have been replaced with purple as they became available. The angel garland, which wore out over time, has occasionally been replaced by something different. And the green and purple ribbons, although I have saved them, have been replaced by a multitude of angel and purple ornaments. Over the years, as I would tell my family and friends about Joey's tree, I would find myself the recipient of beautiful purple or angel ornaments. To all of them, I will always be grateful for helping me and my family through each and every Christmas since Joey passed away.

Some of the ornaments I used on our tree prior to Joey's death, I passed down to Jeremy, since they too have so many wonderful memories attached to them.

Another tradition, John and I do each Christmas is place a live wreath on Joey's grave. Every year if possible, his wreath is adorned with a purple ribbon. It's amazing, although sad, how comforting this tradition also is.

Chapter 20

Joey's Birthday

J oey always felt a little cheated on his birthday, since it fell on December twenty-seventh. He probably did get cheated because it was so close to Christmas.

When Joey was young, we would always have a special birthday party for him and his friends, and then we would have a party for him with our family, usually when we would get together for the holidays.

As Joey got older, we usually would have a birthday cake for him on Christmas or on his birthday if possible.

But this year, 2000, there would be no party, no cake, or so I thought. And even sadder than that, December twenty-seventh, two thousand would have been Joey's twenty-first birthday. He came so close, passing away approximately six months shy of his twenty-first birthday. How could we not celebrate him on that day!

So we decided to have a twenty-first birthday party for Joey. We invited our closest family and Joey's closest friends, including all those who had been so supportive when he died. We ordered a beautiful twenty-first birthday cake. So on that evening, in our dining room, where we had celebrated so many times with Joey, we lit the candles on his cake and sang Happy Birthday to him.

We would continue this birthday tradition for Joey four more times, each year sending out invitations to our closest family and only his closest friends. They were so devoted in attending the party each year. I hope it helped them cope with Joey's death. But it certainly did help me and my family. After five years, and five birthday celebrations for Joey, we decided it was time to stop. But I can only hope that every year on December twenty-seventh, Joey is still in their thoughts and hearts.

Chapter 21

The Anniversary of Joey's Death

When a loved one dies, the anniversary of their death is always sad. But in the case of a child, that day each year can be quite devastating. So as Joey's anniversary approached, June twelfth, I decided I would have to do something, to help us manage to get through that day.

Being Catholic, I decided to have a Mass on that day in Joey's memory. Believe it or not, it was consoling. And so I did that for probably ten years. On that day, I, my sister Tess, my cousin Denise, and sometimes other family members or friends would attend the Mass. Afterwards, some of us would go for breakfast. In the beginning, I would always take that day off from work. That was what I needed to do, to enjoy the company of family and friends, and just take care of myself.

Another thing we started doing on the first anniversary of Joey's death up to today, is putting a memorial in the local newspaper for him, with his high school photo and with something I now personally write. In the beginning, I would use poems or sayings I would find that somehow explained our feelings. But as the years went by, I found it easier to just write something that would come from my heart.

Every year as the day approaches, I get nervous. I fear that this will be the year that I run out of something to say, if that is even possible. Yet every year, as though by Divine Intervention, some wonderful idea seems to pop into my head. I end up writing something which I feel does Joey justice and honors his memory. I have done this for eighteen years now. I wonder if I will ever stop. Maybe never. But I will continue to do this as long as I can, because I know it helps me, John, Jeremy and hopefully other family members and Joey's friends who care, cope with this sad day. The following is what I wrote for the newspaper this year.

In Loving Memory

Dear Joey,

Another year has come and gone, and now it's been eighteen since you left us. Sadly, our lives changed forever on that day. Yet somehow, we've managed to move forward, to live our lives, to be happy. Yet we continue to miss you every second of every day. You will always be our son and brother, and a piece of our hearts will always be with you. So until we meet you again on the other side, we will continue to share your stories, and to cherish all the happy memories we were blessed to make with you. You are always tucked away safely in our hearts. We will love you forever, Joey.

Mom, Dad and Jeremy

Chapter 22

Joey's First Communication with Sabrina

Jeremy really wanted to go on vacation and take his friend Danny with us, the summer right after Joey's death. So we decided a change of scenery would be a good thing for all of us. We didn't want to go far, so we decided to go to Six Flags "Great Adventure" in New Jersey, then down to the Jersey shore, and finish up with "Dorney Park" in Allentown, PA.

Since we used to live in the Allentown area, we still had good friends living down there.

I had been friends with Betty since 1974. I met her after I graduated from college and moved to the Lehigh Valley for a job at an electric power company. We both worked in the same department.

At the time, Betty was moving to a brand-new house out in the country. Four years later, in 1978, John and I moved into our new home, just three and a half miles from Betty. Needless to say, we became best friends and are still so today.

Now back to our vacation in July of 2000. Since we would be staying in Allentown, I decided to check with Betty, to see if she would be home and up for a visit from us. So one afternoon, I made a call, which I didn't know at the time, would change my life forever.

Betty's brother, Jack, had been killed in a motorcycle accident the September before. So after we said our hellos, I asked Betty how her mom was doing. With my heart now aching after Joey's death, I truly understood what her mom was going through. Betty's response was that she was doing alright, especially after what her sister, Sabrina, had told her mom about Jack.

Sabrina was Betty's younger sister. She was quite a bit younger than both Betty and myself, like ten years at least, so I really didn't know her well. I had met her a few times at Betty's house during picnics and such, but that was about it.

So after Betty's comment about Sabrina, I asked her what did Sabrina tell her mom about Jack. This was the gist of the response I got from Betty.

She proceeded to tell me that Sabrina has a special gift that she never told me about. People who had passed away would contact Sabrina, who in turn would give their messages to loved ones they had left behind. Jack had contacted her. The messages he told Sabrina to give to their mom brought her comfort.

So my question for Betty of course was, "Did Sabrina hear anything from Joey?" Betty's answer was yes, but she didn't want to tell me because she didn't want me to feel bad. So I asked her what did Joey tell Sabrina? This is what Betty told me.

Betty and Sabrina had an Aunt Callie, who they both were really close to. When Betty told Aunt Callie that Joey had died, Callie immediately called Sabrina to tell her. Sabrina said that immediately after Callie told her, Joey was in Sabrina's face, so to speak. Joey had died suddenly and unexpectedly and Sabrina shared that he said that he never expected it. Sabrina said that after Joey realized that he had died, and that he was floating over his body, his reaction was like, oh, shit! He told Sabrina to tell John and me that he never expected it. Also he never meant to hurt us. But he wanted us to know that he was alright.

Chapter 23

Our Shared Beliefs

*A*fter *my phone call with Betty, I definitely felt some relief. I told* John and Jeremy, and my sister Tess, what Sabrina had said. I think my biggest relief was that Joey said that he was alright. And for the first time that age old question, is there anything after death, was answered for me by Joey. His body may have died, but his soul lived on. That was huge for me!

Joey and I were really very much alike. We were both quiet and on the shy side until we got to know you. After that, we were chatty and outgoing.

We both also believed in spirits and the supernatural. We had many discussions about what might happen after we die. Joey believed in God, and in heaven and hell.

Joey was my scary movie buddy. I remember watching scary movies with him as far back as when he was around eleven. I was the same way growing up. I would love to watch horror movies, peeking at the movie or TV screen between my fingers.

We both waited eagerly for the movie, "The Sixth Sense[7]" to come out on video. I remember the day it did. I reserved it at Price Chopper, to pick up on my way home from work. Joey called me to see if I could rent it. Happily, I told him I already had. I came home that day with the movie and a large pizza. John, Joey and I watched it together. Soon after it was over, Jeremy came home from football practice, and all four of us watched it again.

For all these reasons, it was no surprise for me, that Joey found Sabrina to let us know that he was alright. He knew for sure I would believe and accept what Sabrina told me.

Chapter 24

Our First Vacation After Joey Passed

In Joey's lifetime we had taken a few vacations without him. One time, we went up to Lake George, and Joey stayed with his best friend, also named Jeremy, in the Lehigh Valley. Another time, my son Jeremy and I vacationed in Orlando, Florida, while John and Joey stayed home. Needless to say, this vacation without Joey was different. He was truly gone and we would never enjoy his company on vacation again.

I remember sitting on a bench by myself at Six Flags "Great Adventure" in Jackson Township, New Jersey, our first destination. John, Jeremy and Jeremy's friend Danny were out and about in the park. I remember that my body just ached from head to toe. My heart was so heavy, I just wanted to die.

Our last vacation stop was "Dorney Park and Wild Water Kingdom" in Allentown, PA. We had gone there many times with Joey and Jeremy when we lived near Allentown. We used to love going to the park after supper with the kids during the week in the summertime. It was cheaper to get in and not very crowded. They always had a great time!

I think it was now our last full day of our mini vacation. We would be going home the next day. We had all been at the park that day. John and I were ready to leave, but the two guys weren't. Since we were staying at a hotel right across the road from the park, and since the guys were fifteen, we felt comfortable leaving them by themselves. They would come back to the hotel when they had enough of the Park.

I called my friend Betty to see if she and her family would be home in the early evening, so John and I could visit. So after the guys returned to our hotel room and we ate dinner, John and I left for Betty's.

It had rained that day in the country where Betty lived, but not in Allentown. So the sky was one of those funky skies, that sometimes happens after a storm. Parts of the sky were dark and cloudy, while others were sunny and bright. As we rode up the highway on our way to Betty's, I looked out our car window, and noticed a brilliant rainbow in the sky. Even in all my sadness, it brought a tiny ray of happiness into my heart. John either didn't see it or didn't comment on it, and I just remained silent.

As soon as we arrived at Betty's house, we were greeted by her running out the door, telling me that her sister Sabrina was on "AOL Instant Messenger," on Betty's computer. Joey was contacting Sabrina and she wanted to talk to me. So I ran into Betty's spare bedroom where they kept their computer, and began my online conversation with Sabrina that would continue to change my life forever.

She said that Joey said he was fine. He said, "Mom, it's beautiful here, beautiful colors, and animals." He said, "Mom,

I can fly, I really can fly!" Sabrina also said spirits of animals that have passed on are also there.

Joey said he was worried about me getting ill. He didn't want that to happen. He sensed nocturnal tears. I told Sabrina that's because I cry every night before I fall asleep. She said that was probably it. But she said that Joey was telling her that he holds my hand every night when I'm sleeping. She said he said he'll come to me in my dreams.

He said he loves his brother Jeremy very much. He said Jeremy probably feels like he abandoned him, but he didn't. He said he hangs out with Jeremy in his room at night. Sabrina said that Joey feels like Jeremy's protector and will be.

Then Joey said he tried to be what he thought we wanted him to be, but it was just too hard with all of his addictions. But he said he was fine now.

He said to tell his dad John, that he tried to be what he wanted him to be, but he couldn't. But tell his dad that he loved him and admired him.

Then Sabrina said she was getting messages from Joey about who helped him pass over. She said she was getting images of a male spirit who had passed over, but who had been at Joey's baptism. I told her my dad, Joey's grandfather, and John's brother, Joey's uncle had both died before Joey, but had both been at Joey's baptism. Sabrina said the baptism could also be a sign of a new beginning. Then she said she sensed it was an older male spirit. Then Sabrina asked me if I knew anyone called Pop Pop who had passed on. I remembered my niece Katie had called my Dad, Poppy. Then

Sabrina asked me if an older male spirit Joey knew had cancer.
I told her that my dad had a lymphoma when he died.
Sabrina said that was it. It was my dad, Joey's grandfather,
who had been waiting for him and helped him cross over. In
fact, Sabrina said my dad was with him at that moment, and
that he had his arm around Joey. Joey said my dad just patted
me on the head. Joey said he would be with me and would
be my guardian angel.

Sabrina said she also sensed an older dog spirit by Joey's
side, a medium sized dog. She asked me if Joey had a dog
that had passed on. Of course, Jake, our old English sheep
dog came to mind. We had him when Joey was born and had
to put him to sleep when Jake was fifteen and Joey was about
eleven. Sabrina said that's probably the dog by Joey's side.

Joey also told me to let his dad John grieve in his own
way. He also told me not to be afraid to lean on John. He
wanted a circle of love in our house.

Joey said he was also very touched by all the people who
were at his funeral service. He didn't realize so many people
cared about him.

Joey also told Sabrina that he can interrupt electric
frequencies, like lights and radios, so to watch for such signs.

Sabrina also asked me if I went for walks. I said I walked
all the time. She said Joey wanted to tell me that he would be
walking with me.

Joey also said he didn't suffer when he died. He just
slipped away.

My intense online conversation with Sabrina was winding
down, when she said that there was one last thing that Joey

wanted to tell me. Wiping away the deluge of tears after such an overwhelming experience, I asked her what that was. She told me that Joey wanted her to tell me that HE WOULD SEND ME RAINBOWS! I had not mentioned to Sabrina or anyone, the rainbow I had seen earlier. All I could think at that moment was that not even death could destroy the bond of love that Joey and I shared.

Chapter 25

Our Return Home

*O*ur brief vacation had been bittersweet. Jeremy was only fifteen and needed to have fun. But it was sad, knowing Joey would never be a part of any vacations again.

After we returned home, we tried to resume our lives the best we could. John had already returned to work. Jeremy was trying to enjoy his summer. I was still home from work. Joey's death really hit me hard!

While we had been away my only sibling, my sister Tess, had come to our house daily to take care of our dog Fred, and cat Cinnamon. While in our house, she said she often smelled a fragrance, like men's cologne. She also shared that while in her house, which was only about ten years old at the time, she witnessed a peculiar occurrence. She said her bedroom door, when not closed tightly, would creep open a bit by itself. She would shut it, although not tightly. Later she would notice that it had crept open again a few inches by itself. Her bedroom door had never done this before.

She shared the fragrance and door occurrences with me, because she thought both were odd. I emailed Sabrina about them. She said Joey told her it was him. Sabrina said that after people have died, they sometimes send such messages through smells, objects moving, interrupting electrical frequencies and so on, to let those they left behind know that they are okay. Joey said he was sending such messages to his aunt that he was okay.

Chapter 26

Messages From Beyond
("Blair Witch Project")

*J*oey *would continue to send me messages through Sabrina, or through* unusual occurrences that I or others would experience. And Sabrina and I began an almost daily back and forth communication about Joey through emails.

In the beginning, Joey would tell her things to tell me that would comfort me. For example, he told her to tell me not to listen to people who would say things like, "poor, poor Joey!" She said that he said not to feel sorry for him. He said it was his time to go and that he was alright.

After he first died, he told her that the place where he was, was so beautiful! He said the colors were so different than any he had ever seen. They were so vibrant beyond belief!

Another time, Joey told Sabrina to tell me to remember the good times we shared together, like a movie Joey and I had seen in the movies together. Sabrina said he told her that it was very scary or very unusual. At first, I didn't remember any such movie. However, soon after this, I was looking through some of my mementos that I had saved. As I went through them, I came across two ticket stubs I didn't remember I had saved. They were for a movie called "The Blair Witch Project.[8]" I had forgotten that Joey and I had gone to see it back in July, 1999. It was on a Saturday, and I had just dropped off my ID badge at a company I was leaving in order to start working full time at a communications company. Joey had seen the movie the night before with friends. Knowing how much I also loved horror films, he said, "Mom, you have to see it!" So on that special Saturday in July, Joey and I went to see an afternoon viewing of "The Blair Witch Project." It was both unusual and scary! We shared a wonderful afternoon which I will remember forever.

Chapter 27

Joey's Ring

O ne day *Sabrina told me that Joey told her to tell me to look for his* ring that he had left behind. For the life of me, I didn't remember a ring Joey owned. He didn't have a high school ring, because he didn't really care if he had one. He said he couldn't justify spending so much money on one.

So one day, I decided to start looking through Joey's belongings, to try to figure out what he was talking about. I cried as I looked through his things. But lo and behold, I soon found the ring Joey wanted me to find. One I had forgotten we had given him.

Joey was probably still in middle school, which was, at the time, fifth through eighth grade. I don't remember his exact age. Joey said that he would like a gold ring with a diamond in it. So it was a birthday gift, since Joey's birthday was December twenty-seventh. Always being on a budget, I bought him a ring as close to his wish as possible, since that's what moms do. It was a 10k gold ring, with his initial J engraved on it. And in the middle of the face of the ring was a diamond chip. He was thrilled when he opened up the package!

It was so nice to find his ring! But what's even more amazing is that Joey saved it. Having addictions, Joey sold many things to get money, a starter guitar we had bought him, a few gaming systems, and so on. But he didn't sell his ring! I choose to believe he didn't because it was our gift to him and it was special. The fact that he instructed Sabrina to have me look for it, seals the deal for me. I wear it often, when I'm going out. It helps me feel like Joey is with me. Otherwise, I keep it in a safe place. I plan on giving it to Jeremy someday, if I can ever part with it. Jeremy also told me that it is so precious to him, that he would probably keep it locked up in a safe.

Chapter 28

Butterflies

*B*utterflies are so lovely. I had always gotten a happy feeling whenever I was fortunate enough to see one. However, I could never have guessed that one little butterfly would change my life forever.

Soon after Joey passed away, I started again to take daily walks down at two lovely parks not far from our house. I had become quite the walker in the last few years, and walking always seemed to pick me up when I was feeling down. There's a lot to be said for endorphins.

The parks where I continue to occasionally walk to this day are so great! The two separate parks are divided by a river. On one side of the river is the park in Valleytown. The park on the other side of the river is in O Town. O Town is actually the town where I grew up. The parks are connected by a steel/wooden planked foot bridge that goes over the river. Both parks are great! The Valleytown Park has circular paved walking trails, tennis and basketball courts, baseball and soccer fields. It is also next door to an elementary school and high school football field. My son, Jeremy, attended that elementary school and played football on that field. So no matter what time you walk there, there's usually some action going on. But what I like most about this park is that a small mulched branch of the trail runs along the river. Not only do you enjoy the beauty of nature as you walk along it, but also occasionally encounter some beautiful wildlife and interesting humans. I've seen swimming ducks, flying blue cranes, fishermen in the water, and kayaks going down the river.

The O Town Park is just as quaint! The walking trails are mostly mulched. They meander up and down small inclines through the woods, along railroad tracks, around baseball and football fields, and along the bank of the river. Not only is it an exhilarating walk, but it is always interesting and beautiful. As you walk, you enjoy the trees and the foliage as they change through the seasons, and occasionally run into a rabbit or squirrel, or even a deer. One time I came upon a doe and her two fawns.

Now that I've set the scene, back to butterflies. One dreary, drizzly morning, soon after Joey passed, I decided to take my chances and go for a walk down the parks. I hoped the walk would at least help me feel better. Cheering me up was not even a possibility at that point in my life. I decided to take the path right along the river in the Valleytown Park. As I did, I suddenly noticed this beautiful, colorful monarch butterfly. It was especially spectacular as it sat on some lovely pink flowers against the backdrop of a dark and dreary day. I gazed at the brilliant oranges and blacks and intricate white dots on its wings. But the unusual part was that it just sat there motionless on the flower, as if it was allowing me to take in its beauty, in order to help comfort me in my grief. So as it sat there, I snapped its photo with my camera, which I had started bringing along with me on my walks. I thanked God that I had it with me on that day.

When I returned home, I decided to send Sabrina an email about my encounter with the butterfly. Emails to her had become a daily ritual. Needless to say, as always, her response did lift my spirits. She told me that butterflies were very significant. She said that some believe they are symbols of rebirth or new life. Seeing that butterfly she felt, was a symbol of Joey's rebirth/new life at wherever we go after we die. From that moment on, I would never look at a butterfly in the same light again. To me, a butterfly would always be a sign or reminder from Joey, that he was okay.

My photo of this butterfly was spectacular! I blew it up and framed it. It still hangs on our living room wall.

Chapter 29

Electrical Interference

One afternoon after Joey died, I was on our computer which was on the upstairs balcony of our house. In the ceiling of the balcony was a large whole house ceiling fan built right into the ceiling. If you turned it on in warm weather, it would do a good job of pulling the hot air out of the house and out the attic vents. It was great, since we didn't have central air conditioning. It worked almost as good. But the fan could be noisy if you turned it on high.

It was very warm that summer day, so I had the fan on the medium setting. As I was doing something right there on the computer, all of a sudden, the fan stopped. Remembering that Joey had told Sabrina that he could interrupt electrical frequencies affecting the operation of, for example, lights and radios, I said, "Joey, is that you?" The fan stayed off for maybe a few minutes. I got up to check whether the fan was on or off, but it was still on the medium setting. Then it started again on its own. I never touched it. A few minutes later it stopped again, same as before. I said, "Joey, are you with me?" I got up, checked the clocks upstairs and then downstairs, to see if they were flashing as they did when there was a total power interruption in the house. But they were not; plus, my computer was working normally. Finally, a few minutes later, the fan started by itself a second time. I never touched the switch. I knew in my heart it was Joey.

I mentioned this occurrence to Sabrina the next time I emailed her. This is what she told me. "Well, I think Joey is getting through to you... The fan going off and on is a sure sign of a spirit in your home, especially at a time when you're upset...Turning it off once is the sign to get your attention, and then the second time is the confirmation. That's how it works a lot of times if you have doubt."

I never doubted it again that Joey was okay and that he had communicated with me. In fact, after having told my husband John and my son Jeremy about it, the same scenario occurred a second time when Jeremy and I were on the balcony that summer. That's another story to tell.

Chapter 30

Best Friends

*J*oey *was born in December, 1979. At the time we lived in our first* house, which we built and moved into in September 1978. It was in a rural community about fifteen miles outside of Allentown, Pennsylvania. Joey spent the first ten and a half years of his life there.

Probably around the age of five, when Joey started kindergarten, he met our neighbor named Jeremy Esson. Jeremy Esson was Joey's age. His house was on a street in our neighborhood on the top of a hill. You could see his house from the back of ours, and the back of their property which was hilly fields, butted against the back of our yard.

In no time they became best friends. Jeremy Esson's mom had a horse farm, and the horses would graze in the fields behind our yard. Joey and Jeremy would often go back and forth to each other's house, climbing up and down those hills. Joey would be a little scared passing the horses, but I guess he got used to it.

They spent many a waking hour together. They went to school and played together, played baseball and soccer together, and took karate classes together. They were inseparable.

One of the most incredible things they shared together, was the birth of one of Jeremy's mom's horse's foals. One night, very, very late, Jeremy called Joey to tell him to come up to the barn to witness the birth. Joey and John ran up and did witness the miracle event. Both said it was awesome!

However, one of the saddest outcomes of our move back to Northeastern Pennsylvania in 1990 to be near our families, was that Joey and Jeremy Esson would have to part ways. Before we moved, one of Jeremy's parents took a photo of Joey and Jeremy together. Jeremy held his two fingers up behind Joey's head to look like two horns. They gave Joey a framed copy of that photo as a going away present. After our move, Joey would sleep with that photo in his arms for a very long time. He so missed Jeremy.

We finally moved into our new house in April, 1991. We had been living with my mom in her house while ours was being built. Joey and Jeremy Esson visited each other periodically after we moved. We would meet halfway off the Pennsylvania Turnpike for the kid drop off. When we finally moved into our house, Jeremy came to visit. John took an updated photo of Joey and Jeremy together. This time it was Joey putting his two fingers behind Jeremy's head. We gave Jeremy his framed copy. Both photos still adorn our house. The smiles on their faces in both photos still warm my heart. They are the smiles of true friendship. Joey and Jeremy remained in touch and visited periodically until Joey passed away in 2000. We still keep in touch with Jeremy Esson who is now married and the father of a little boy. He and his family will always be special members of our family.

So now that you know the importance of Jeremy Esson in Joey's life, you will be able to appreciate the following story.

One summer day after Joey passed, I took out a box of belongings from Joey's bedroom closet, that he had saved. My son Jeremy was home, so he and I started looking through Joey's things. As we lovingly handled what was in the box, we came across an essay that Joey had obviously written for school, probably in the fifth grade, his first school year in his new school. It was written in Joey's cursive handwriting. This is what it said.

"My Neighbor"

"My neighbor is my best friend. We ride bikes together. One day we went into tunnels under the road that the water goes in. We got all wet. When we got home, we told my mom that we fell in a puddle. My neighbor's name is Jeremy Esson. He has horses. We rode one and its name is Flash."

Jeremy and I could not believe the treasure we had stumbled upon. I knew I would be sending it to Jeremy Esson. As we sat on the floor of our balcony, enjoying our discovery, we suddenly heard a bang in the bathroom in my bedroom. It startled us! We ran into the bathroom to see what had fallen. There on the floor sat my white plastic butterfly that had fallen off my bathroom wall. But it wasn't broken. The hook on the back of the butterfly which was just white hard plastic, was also plastic just molded right into the butterfly's body. Nothing had broken. All was still intact. The nail it was hung on was also still securely in the wall. It was as though someone just lifted the butterfly off the nail and let it fall to the floor. In addition, there were two butterflies hanging on the wall but only one fell.

Jeremy and I just looked at each other. We chose to believe that Joey was just giving us a sign of his approval of our discovery, and letting us know that he was alright.

Chapter 31

My First Reiki Session

A few months after Joey passed, in the summer of 2000, I decided to take another trip down to my friend Betty's. After what she had told me about Sabrina's gift, and after what I had experienced, I decided to schedule a session with Sabrina. Through email, Sabrina explained to me that my session with her would be a Reiki session. I had never heard about Reiki, which at the time was relatively unknown to many. She told me that she had taken Reiki training and was now certified to do it. She explained what it was to me. Not exactly remembering her explanation, I looked Reiki up online and found this definition. It is "a healing technique based on the principle that the therapist can channel energy into the patient by means of touch, to activate the natural healing processes of the patient's body and restore physical and emotional well-being."

After Sabrina's explanation of Reiki, she also continued to tell me that sometimes, because of her special gift, people who had passed would communicate or channel through her to the person whom she was performing Reiki on. She told me however, that you never really could count on that happening. Also if someone did come through, it could be someone who may have known you or known someone who knew you. They may want you to communicate to someone else. So basically, she didn't want me to get my hopes up that Joey might come through.

She did advise me however to bring a few personal belongings of Joey's with me. Sometimes this did help to have a certain person come through.

After hearing this, I decided I really had to put a lot of thought into which belongings of Joey's I would bring with me.

So which belongings should I take with me? Picking something that had really meant a lot to him was important to me.

I know I decided on a few items, but the most relevant one was the purple Kung Fu sash Joey had earned. This is why I chose it.

When Joey was a little guy, probably five or six, he and his best friend Jeremy Esson had taken karate together. Joey had earned a few belts, yellow, orange, green. But after a year or two, he grew tired of it and quit. Jeremy Esson however, went on to become a black belt.

So approximately thirteen/fourteen years later, in the summer of 1999, when Joey was nineteen, he and his friend Pete, decided to enroll in Kung Fu. I was thrilled! After about two years of battling his addictions, Joey seemed to be turning things around. I was all for his renewed interest in the martial arts.

Joey went on to earn a few Kung Fu sashes, a yellow one being his first, and the purple being his last. These were milestones for Joey, because a lot of learning and training are required before testing for each sash. He threw his heart and soul into it. We were all so very proud of him, as he was of himself. The whole experience was great for Joey. It gave him direction. He also became a member of this Kung Fu family, and he cherished that and all the wonderful friendships that came out of it. He truly felt that he belonged.

So my mind was made up! I would take Joey's purple sash with me. Since it was the last and highest ranked sash he had earned, I felt in my heart it probably was the most important to him also. My sister Tess volunteered to go with me to Betty's house for my first Reiki session with Sabrina. I wasn't sure what to expect, but needless to say, I was excited with the hope that maybe Joey would speak to me through Sabrina.

After a lovely lunch with Betty, Sabrina and their mom and Aunt Callie at a local pizza restaurant, we made our way to Betty's.

It was decided that my session would be in Betty's finished basement which is lovely, quiet and private. Everyone else would chat upstairs.

Before my session began, Sabrina asked me if I had brought any of Joey's belongings. I showed and gave them to her. All I told her about Joey's purple sash was that it was the last one he earned before he died. I laid down on Betty's couch and Sabrina began the session.

There were many things that happened during that incredibly emotional Reiki session. Some of what was said has faded over the years, but Joey did come through and gave me the following messages.

He reiterated not to feel sorry for him, but that it was his time to go. He told Sabrina again, for me to remember the good times we shared together.

As for the purple sash I brought along with me, Joey explained the following. Remember, I gave Sabrina no explanation of its significance, I did not mention his yellow sash at all. All she knew is that it was Joey's.

Joey said he was proud that he earned his last sash, the purple one. However, he was proudest that he earned his first, the yellow sash. He said the yellow sash was more special because he worked the hardest for it. He proved to himself that he could make a fresh start and turn his life around. And that's exactly what he was doing that summer of 1999.

All of Joey's Kung Fu sashes are now tucked safely away with other important mementos of his. I was always so proud of him for earning all his sashes because I knew how difficult it was for him. But after what Joey told me about his first yellow sash through Sabrina, well, I was just blown away! He had never confided these feelings to me when he was alive, but how wonderful to learn about them, even if after his death.

Chapter 32

"With Arms Wide Open"

During the week between Christmas 1999, Joey's last Christmas with us, and New Year's 2000, my son Jeremy and I went on vacation with my sister Tess and her family to Florida. Joey could've come, but for whatever reason he wanted to stay home with John.

Jeremy had gotten a camcorder on that Christmas and took it on vacation. Earlier, he had recorded our annual Christmas day get-together with our family at our house. He was able to record most of our vacation until his camcorder was stolen on December 31, 1999 at Universal Studios, where we were waiting for their New Year's Eve fireworks. Jeremy, with his camcorder by his side, and I were sitting on the steps of the Hard Rock Café, waiting for the fireworks. We were both pretty exhausted after having spent the entire day at the park. I noticed a table with chairs on the patio became available. I ran to grab the seats thinking we would be more comfortable. So as I yelled to Jeremy, he followed me, sat down, but immediately remembered his camcorder. Literally, less than a minute later, he ran back to retrieve it from the steps, but it was gone. Someone had taken it!

Jeremy was heartbroken. His and my vacation pretty much ended at that moment. We reported the incident to Universal lost and found, left our information, but it was never returned. That night I remember, Jeremy and I called home to wish John and Joey a Happy New Year, and to tell them what had happened. As I spoke to Joey, I remember him telling me how sad he was for Jeremy, what a good kid he was, and how he didn't deserve this.

After we returned home, our insurance company did reimburse us, so that Jeremy was able to get a new camcorder, but the videos he had taken couldn't be replaced. We assumed our Christmas video, our last one with Joey, was gone.

At the time of that 1999 Christmas, a song was popular, "With Arms Wide Open[9]" by the band Creed, with lead singer, Scott Stapp. I really loved the song. I said it reminded me of Pearl Jam. Jeremy said no. But for whatever reason, both Jeremy and I agreed it reminded us of Joey.

After Joey passed in June, 2000, I asked Jeremy if he had any video of the previous Christmas that may have survived, and not been taken to Florida. He said no. I think maybe he was just too heartbroken to check.

But one day that summer, as I sat on the couch in our family room, Jeremy came running downstairs all excited. He had found the Christmas tape and Joey was on it.

As we watched the video, which was kind of bittersweet, we were able to enjoy again our last Christmas with Joey. You could tell he was very happy and enjoying his time with his family. So as we watched the end of the tape, it showed Joey in our dining room with some of us, being silly, holding his Barbie sized Bruce Lee Doll,[10] Joey's idol, in his hands, and moving the doll's arms and legs to do Kung Fu moves. But as I watched Joey on the video, suddenly Jeremy told me to listen to the song playing in the background. So I did, "With Arms Wide Open." Enough said!

Chapter 33

Massage Therapy

During the summer of 2000, immediately after Joey died, I began noticing a lot of television commercials about starting a career as a massage therapist. I had never had a massage myself, but it seemed like a great way to help people. I had gone back to school about seventeen years earlier to earn my Master's Degree in Elementary Education, and eventually changed careers for a few years. So I thought maybe I could do it again.

As with my prior schooling for my education degree, I decided that if I could continue to work my current full-time day, Monday through Friday job, and attend massage school nights and/or weekends, I would consider it. At the time there was one local school where I could do this. I seriously considered it, but decided it may be too much for me emotionally in 2000. But the seed had been sown.

So about a year later, in August of 2001, I began my massage schooling, Monday through Thursday evenings. I graduated in November of 2002. I was happy that I had put it off for a year. Some of the courses were pretty challenging! The most difficult for me was Kinesiology.

So from 2002 until 2010, I continued working at my full-time office job, but also worked several massage therapy jobs over the years. Some were on the weekends, some were at night. Finally in 2010, I was able to leave my office job and pursue massage therapy full time.

Although working as a massage therapist is physically demanding, mentally and emotionally, it is one of the best decisions I have ever made! So I don't know who planted that seed in my brain back in 2000. I would like to think it was Joey, still looking out for me, because quite frankly, the idea came out of nowhere. There was no rhyme or reason to it.

After Joey's death, going through the massage therapy program kept my mind extremely busy and focused, thus less time to ponder his absence. I believe it was somehow what I needed at the time. In a sense it gave me a purpose to continue on, something to look forward to. It distracted me at least a bit, during the darkest days of my life. But the best part is I finally found an amazing profession where I can help people. I found my niche!

So for the last sixteen plus years, I have worked as a massage therapist at resorts, spas, rehabilitation centers and chiropractic offices. All of these positions have helped me advance my skills, plus allowed me to do something I really love.

Over the years, I've given massages definitely to hundreds of people, probably thousands. In this capacity I've come to believe that sometimes I'm brought to a person because they need me at that point in time. Other times they're brought to me because I need them. With this in mind, I would like to share a massage session I will never forget.

It was probably about six years after Joey died and I was working at a spa. My client, Andrea, had been in a car accident. She came for massage on a regular basis.

Sometimes I chit chat with my client during their session, if that is what they like. If you have enough sessions with the person, you tend to cover a lot of topics.

After many sessions we did somehow get on the topic of children, so she did know that Joey died. At one point she told me her dad was very ill and in the hospital.

One session when she arrived, she informed me that her dad had passed away quietly in the hospital. But she was a bit disappointed that he left with no fanfare. She said he was quite the character! She expected that maybe the door would've slammed shut, or a breeze would've moved the curtains in the hospital room when he died. But there was nothing. In fact, she was surprised that he hadn't sent her any signs at all that he was okay. We both laughed and decided the signs would come. Almost at that exact moment, as she lay face down on the massage table, the room went dark. The light was completely off. I wasn't sure if she could tell because her face was in the face cradle. But she could. So we decided that it was a sign from her dad, or Joey, or both, and that they were okay.

After this happened, I had to physically turn the light switch to turn the light back on. Again, I would like to think that this occurrence was more than just a coincidence.

Chapter 34

Joey's Hair

*W*hen *Joey was probably in seventh or eighth grade, it was early fall* and time for annual school photo day. I enjoyed these photos, because I could see how my kids changed from year to year. This year though was a bit different. Joey had gotten a short haircut at the beginning of the summer, but for whatever reason had now decided to let it grow long. But as it did, it was a bit straggly. As picture day approached, I kept urging Joey to get his hair cut. I told him I would call our hairdresser and make an appointment. But he refused. So the morning of pictures arrived. I bought Joey a new, rather colorful shirt. I loved it and so did he. It had splashes of purple, pinks and so on, kind of like fireworks. He looked great that morning, even with his straggly hair. So off he went.

I went about my business that day. As the time arrived for Joey to come home, he opened up the front door. The first words out of his mouth were, "Mom, call and make me a haircut appointment." I wanted to kill him, of course figurately speaking, but I let it go. I don't know if someone said something to him that day at school, but we never discussed it.

About a week later, Joey brought his photos home from school. He asked me to promise never to show or give these photos to anyone, not his grandmother, not Aunt Tess, not my cousin Denise, not anyone. He also asked me never to display it in our house. So being the Mom I am, I bought the photos anyway. They were beautiful photos of my handsome son Joey with straggly hair. But I never displayed them in our house or gave them to anyone. I kept my promise to Joey. But I still have those photos, and they rank up there with some of my favorites.

So with all that being said, I can now talk about another Reiki session with Sabrina. As most times happens for me, Joey came through. Some, who believe in reincarnation, which I now do, say that between our lives we go to a place where we review our most recent life. There we also continue to grow, learn, and master our skills. Joey loved playing guitar and was very good at it. During this session he told me that he was happy and concentrating on his guitar skills and becoming better. But at the end of the session, as he does many times, he tells Sabrina there's one more thing he wants me to know. He says, "Tell my mom I'm growing my hair long again." So as Sabrina looks at me and asks, "Does this mean anything to you?", holding back tears, I shake my head, yes! What a wonderful possibility!

Chapter 35

Bear Hugs

*A*s Joey got older, and I don't remember why or how it started, he started giving me what he called "Bear Hugs." Joey wasn't a big guy, probably about five feet six inches and of average weight. But he was strong! I remember one time in particular, we were standing by the island in our kitchen, the day he earned his purple sash in Kung Fu. Joey decided to give me a "Bear Hug." He held me so tightly, I had to ask him to let me go because it hurt. Yet I loved those hugs!

I remember one day, I was with one of Joey's best friends, Brad. I guess we were talking about Joey. I also remember telling him, one of the things I missed most was Joey's "Bear Hugs." So Brad walked over to me and said, "I'll give you a Bear Hug." And so he did.

So again at the end of one of my Reiki sessions with Sabrina, as she's telling me Joey's messages, she tells me to stay still and close my eyes. Then she says, "Did you feel it? Joey just gave you a 'Bear Hug.'" As I opened up my teary eyes, I asked her what did she mean, a "Bear Hug?" She said all she could see was Joey with his arms wide open, and then closing them tightly as if giving me a big hug!

Chapter 36

Doogan

*B*ack *in December, 1980, for Joey's first Christmas or first birthday,* John's brother, Ken, my brother-in-law, gave Joey this stuffed dog named Doogan. Joey kept the name Doogan because there was a small leather logo on the dog's chest with the name Doogan on it. He is about twenty-two inches tall, and has floppy brown ears. The rest of his body is an orangey color. He also has raised brown plastic eyes that seem to look straight at you, literally "puppy dog eyes." Above his eyes is what I call his flap. If you push the flap up, he looks happy, push it down he looks angry. Well, Joey loved Doogan! He became Joey's favorite stuffed animal.

So one day back in probably around March of 2008, I remember lying in bed one night and suddenly thinking about Doogan, out of the blue! Where was Doogan? We had moved twice since Joey died, so I decided Doogan must have gotten lost in the shuffle. So about two weeks after that, my friend Emma, who I spoke of earlier, and I made plans to meet for lunch on a Sunday afternoon. Now and then we do that. I remember the year was 2008, because Emma was expecting her first child. I remember buying a few little gifts for the baby, even though I would be going to her baby shower in a few weeks.

We both drove our own cars to the restaurant. I left the gifts in my car trunk. I remember the day being very windy and cold. We had a lovely lunch as always. As we were leaving, I told her I had something in my car for her. She said she also had something for me. So we both went to our cars which were parked side by side, and opened our trunks. Lo and behold, she gets Doogan out of her trunk, all nicely wrapped in clear plastic. As I look at him, I'm speechless! Thinking I don't remember him she says, "It's Doogan." Just about sobbing by now, I tell her I do remember but just can't believe my eyes! So I tell her how just two weeks earlier, I was wondering where Doogan was. So Emma tells me her story.

When she and Joey were dating, one day he brings her Doogan. He tells her he wants her to have him because Doogan is his favorite stuffed animal ever!

So years later, she puts away all her stuffed animals, including Doogan, and forgets about them.

Then she says about two weeks ago, around the time I'm thinking of Doogan, she decides to take out her stuffed animals, thinking she may give some of them to her new baby. Lo and behold, she finds Doogan! She looks at her husband and asks, "Do you think I should give Doogan back to Joey's mom?" They both decided yes.

What else needs to be said! We still have Doogan. He sits safely in one of our upstairs bedrooms with other stuffed friends. I look at and even talk to him often, and sometimes give him an occasional but soft "Bear Hug." Thank you, Joey!

Chapter 37

My Sixty-Second Birthday

*A*s *I woke up the morning of my sixty-second birthday, I saw a* picture in my head as if I was still coming out of a dream. It was a specific twenty-dollar Pennsylvania instant lottery ticket. I knew it because I had purchased it on a few occasions. I remembered stories of how people had dreamt about lottery tickets, bought them and then won oodles of money. So I decided I would buy one hoping for a similar result, especially on this significant birthday.

So later that day, on my way to work, I stopped at a market where I often buy tickets and purchased one. Not winning anything and a little disappointed, I went to work. Since it was payday for me, I drove to the credit union after work to deposit my check. But that ticket was still nagging at me. So I decided I would give it one more shot. I almost stopped at a different market but something told me to go back to the one I had been at earlier. So I did. I remember getting back into my car with the ticket, and whispering to Joey to bring me good luck. As I anxiously scratched the ticket, I soon realized I won one thousand dollars! Almost in tears, I went back into the store, filled out the paperwork and received my birthday gift! I shared this story with only a few special people who knew me well. With no opinion from me, the first words out of their mouths were that it was a gift from Joey.

So a few days later on a Saturday morning, I decided to go shopping. At the plaza I was going to, there was a beauty supply store where I could buy massage cream, and a women's clothing store where I could buy a birthday gift for my cousin Denise. Her birthday is a few days after mine and I knew I would be seeing her the next day. I parked in the parking lot of the plaza which contains about six stores. I parked far away from the stores with no cars around me, as I usually do. After I got out of my car, I checked around it, making sure I had parked in the lines, and then proceeded to the stores.

First, I went into the clothing store and purchased a gift for Denise. Next, I purchased my massage cream at the beauty supply store. This entire shopping excursion took less than thirty minutes.

As I walked back to my car, I noticed something on the pavement right behind my car. As I got closer, it appeared to be money. So I picked it up thinking it was probably just a few dollars. I put my packages in the trunk and got into my car. As I looked at the money, I suddenly realized it was four crisp newish one hundred-dollar bills folded over together. Stunned, I didn't know what to do! There were no cars around me. It was like the money fell from the sky.

Needless to say, I still didn't know what to do. If I took the money into one of the stores, I decided they would probably end up keeping it. But as I drove away, I kept looking in the rearview mirror expecting "John Quiñones" from the television show "What Would You Do," following me.[11] I had called John. So when I arrived home, again in tears, I showed him the money. We were both in disbelief!

Later that day, I shared this story with my family. Denise's daughter Carla, who is a lawyer, basically said "Finders Keepers." I guess this made me feel better. But feeling a bit guilty, I did watch the lost and found section of the newspaper for a few weeks. No claims were ever made.

So all this money, a total of fourteen hundred dollars, went into my checking account. It helped pay for a very special family vacation that November. I had been stressing over making the final payment. All this money was truly a gift!

Nothing quite like this has happened since. However, I still believe it was more than just luck.

Chapter 38

Jake and Fred

*O*ne *of the things that Joey has always told me through Sabrina, is* that our beloved dogs, Jake and Fred, are often with him. Jake was our old English Sheepdog that we had from before Joey was born until Joey was about eleven. Jake was sixteen when he passed. Fred was our Sheltie that we had from the time Joey was about seventeen until years after Joey passed. He tells me they are often with me, and that I could literally trip over them. Many times, Joey says, Fred sleeps next to me on my right, and Jake on my left. What a wonderful thought!

So in November, 2011, when I was already living in my current house, where we moved some years after Joey passed, Sabrina visited me. She made a trip with some of her friends to do a vitamin supplement party at my house. It was like a Tupperware Party,[12] except about vitamins, healthy drink mixes and so on. Sabrina brought her dog Sadie with her. Sadie has since passed. Some believe that animals can see spirits. So while the party was going on, Sadie would come into our kitchen, look toward the open doorway into our bedroom, and bark. She kept doing this, but nothing that

Sabrina could do or say, including taking her out in case she had to relieve herself, helped her to stop. Later on, Sabrina confided to me that Sadie was barking at our Sheltie Fred who was living here when he passed. And honestly, he had passed away wrapped up in his cozy blanket, in our kitchen, right next to the doorway into our bedroom. He used to lay there all the time. Sometimes I do think I feel his presence, and even as crazy as it sounds, seem to catch a glimpse of him out of the corner of my eye.

Chapter 39

A Real Trip!

A *few weeks after Sabrina's visit in November, 2011, she and* other friends returned to my house to do a party on essential oils and body wraps. So again, like a Tupperware Party but with oils and wraps. I had again invited a number of close family and friends I thought might be interested.

But before I continue, I have to take a tangent to tell an important story. Sabrina reminds me of a gypsy. She's a very pretty lady who many times dresses flamboyantly with lots of unique jewelry and color in her hair. But she definitely pulls it off. It works for her. So when I explain her to others, I often describe her as a "Real Trip," but in a good, loving way. Definitely she's not like any of my other friends. Of course, I never told her she was a "Real Trip" because I didn't want to offend her, although it probably wouldn't.

So getting back to my oil party story. I remember, I was sitting in the wooden rocking chair in my current living room. Everyone was abuzz, doing the wraps and chit chatting. Sabrina had been upstairs in our house, using the restroom to wash her hands. After she came back down, she came over to me and scooted herself onto the rocking chair next to me. She quietly began to tell me that she had just seen and been talking to Joey in one of our upstairs bedrooms. She said he told her that he was happy she was my friend because she made me laugh. Then he looked at her and said, "You're a Real Trip!" As she asked me as always if that made sense to me, with tears of joy running down my face, I said, "Yes!"

Chapter 40

Spirit Mist

One night a few months after Joey passed, as I was lying in bed in our home, a weird occurrence happened. I had been thinking of Joey all day, and needless to say, was very sad. After a while, I noticed the bedroom appeared to be getting foggy. Thinking it was because I had been crying, I made sure I wiped the tears from my eyes a few times. But even after that, the fog remained. I would have to say it lasted for about fifteen minutes.

The next day I told Sabrina about it and she explained it was "spirit mist." She said it means someone you love who has passed is near you. She said last night Joey and my dad were near me, and that my dad even gave me a kiss.

Most recently in our current house, I started seeing what I felt was also "spirit mist." Our bedroom is on the first floor, but is open with no doors separating it from the other rooms. So only the stairway to our upstairs and that wall, separates our bedroom and the first floor living room. There is a landing at the bottom of the stairs, with one side step into the bedroom and one side step into the living room. I began noticing this fog in the middle of the living room and at the bottom landing of the stairs. It didn't just happen one time, but many. I would see the mist at the landing when I was in bed or walked down the stairs. I would see the mist in the living room as I walked there or up the stairs. It's funny, but a certain feeling will come over me now when I see this mist. I'll always say or think, "Joey or Mom or Dad, if that is you, I miss you and love you."

So again, I am having another session with Sabrina, and as always telling her nothing. She said nowadays, since Joey has been coming to her for such a long time, they are like friends. The night before I'm coming for a session, she'll meditate. Joey comes to her. She knows what he looks like because they sit and talk face to face. This time they were both sitting on a grassy knoll talking to each other.

She said Joey wanted to tell me that he visits our current house often. He usually hangs out in the middle of the living room or at the bottom of the stairs. She asked if I felt him there. So of course, I then told her what I suspected because of the "spirit mist."

I continue to see the "mist" very often in many places in our house now. When I do, I truly believe Joey is with us, and sometimes maybe my Mom or Dad. It seems it will appear when I need it the most, like on a day when I'm missing Joey terribly. It's as though he's telling me, "Don't worry, Mom. I'm here with you. I love you." I choose to believe that.

Recently, I was talking to a friend who lost her sibling years ago, around the time Joey died. I often tell her my stories about Joey because I know she appreciates them, having lost her loved one at an early age. When I was telling her my stories about "spirit mist," her unexpected question surprised me. She asked "What is that?" She confided she has also experienced it. It was wonderful to discover that she too had seen it. So I finished my stories and told her what I believed. She was excited! I brought up the possibility that when she sees it, maybe her sibling is near. She was happy and hopeful for that.

When I see "spirit mist," there's certainly the chance it may signify nothing, but I continue to believe otherwise.

Chapter 41

A New Messenger

A few years ago, a client at my office named Susan, told a coworker of mine during a private conversation that she was a medium. She shared with her that she had this gift from the time she was a little girl. Susan's mentor suggested to her that she should consider giving readings to people, as a way of giving back and using her gift productively. Well, as soon as we all found this out, we were in!

I'll never forget the day. It was around Thanksgiving and I went to Susan for a reading. Being used to Sabrina and the way she had become so experienced in doing her readings with me, I sort of expected the same with Susan.

So as we sat down in Susan's living room, with a small table between us, she asked me if I had any questions. I answered no. Then she asked me if I wanted her to read my cards. I said not really. So finally, probably a bit frustrated, she told me I was making it really difficult for her. So I quickly apologized, and explained Sabrina to her, and shared that I was accustomed to the way she did her readings.

So after I shared that information with her, she looked at me and asked if I had a young man in my life who had died. So of course, I said, "Yes, my son Joey." At that moment, she told me that Joey was there with us. He told her to tell me he's doing well, and that he is with me often. Not only was he with us, but he also told her he just gave me a "big hug!" She shared that he was standing right behind me, with his left hand on my left shoulder, and his right hand on my right shoulder. Not only did he stand in front of my spirit guides, but also in front of a long line of other spirits behind them. But Susan said Joey turned around and said to all of them, something to the effect, "Get back, this is my Mom and I will take care of her!"

Joey continued that he also looks out for his brother Jeremy, who will be fine. He said Jeremy will do well in life. This was a sentiment Joey shared often with me about Jeremy, even before his death. Joey went on to say that he looks out for a "girl friend." I'm sure he meant Emma. Lastly, Joey shared that he will leave pennies for me and Jeremy, so we'll know he's with us.

So even though on that day, my messenger was Susan and not Sabrina, Joey managed to find his way to me. It was an uplifting experience! I'm not sure if Susan continued to do readings, but my reading that day was amazing! It certainly cemented my belief that Joey's soul continues to exist, and that is with us often.

Chapter 42

With Us In Spirit

When your loved one dies, you miss every little thing about them. You miss their eyes looking at you, their laugh, their kisses and hugs. You miss the conversations with them telling you what's going on in their lives. You miss their voice on the phone. And one of the things that saddens me the most, is that they're not here to celebrate the special joyous occasions with us, the births, holidays and weddings for example.

So recently I was talking to my sister Tess on the phone, and I shared that I was writing this book. I didn't realize that I hadn't told her that I had been working on writing it for ten plus years.

Tess was so excited! And it was so heartwarming for me to discover how much she remembered those years, and all the things I had done to try to get through them. She was and always will be one of my rocks in life. She is always there when I need her.

So we started reminiscing about many of the events that had happened over the years. Then she reminded me of one really special happy occasion which I would like to share. Just keep in mind how some say and how I believe, that our loved ones who have passed are with us in spirit. I and others believe they will send us signs like butterflies, to let us know they are with us.

About four years ago, my favorite and only niece, my only sister's only daughter Katie, got married on a beach in Maui. It was spectacular! She and her fiancé Tom had given us at least two years notice about the wedding. So we all planned and saved for it. I'd say about fifteen close family members and friends made the trip. We did a seven-day cruise around the Hawaiian Islands, flying to and leaving from Honolulu. It was in November, the week before Thanksgiving. Our first stop would be a few days in Maui, so that's where they decided to get married.

It was an absolutely beautiful day and service! Katie and Tom incorporated many Hawaiian customs into their ceremony. It was truly a once in a lifetime event, and I'm so happy that I, John and Jeremy were there to share in the celebration. Of course, in my mind, I wished Joey was there, but I reminded myself that he would be there with us in spirit.

So at one point in the ceremony they released butterflies, which are a symbol of new life, new beginning, very appropriate for a wedding. As they did, the butterflies fluttered about and began to fly off. But one of the butterflies flitted about my niece, then flew from her and landed on Jeremy's face, and sat there long enough for the photographer to snap a picture of that special moment. Well, as you can imagine, there was only one thought that went through my mind and those of my family, with whom I had shared my beliefs. We all agreed Joey had sent us a sign that indeed he was with us to celebrate his only first cousin's marriage.

As a gift that Christmas, Katie and Tom gave Jeremy a framed photo of that special moment in Maui. What a treasure!

Most recently we were at Katie's house for her fortieth birthday party. It was a great time with lots of people, food and live entertainment. I was sitting downstairs in the family room, enjoying the entertainment and talking with my sister Tess and her friend Jackie. For whatever reason, Tess shares with Jackie that I'm writing a book. One thing led to another and of course Jackie was interested in my book. So as I started telling her about Joey and what had happened, all of a sudden, the power went out in the house. The lights and music were gone and there was silence. So someone yelled to Tom, asking him if this had ever happened before. Nervously, he yelled back no! Seconds later, the power came back on. Again, maybe just coincidence, but I'd like to believe that Joey wanted us to know he was with us in spirit, sharing this special occasion.

Chapter 43

Our Journey Continues

And so our unexpected journey without Joey continues. We have all managed to find happiness in our lives. John, who is also now sixty-six years old, plans on working full time another two years. I plan on working part time at least another two years. After that, we'll play it by ear. We are currently planning a trip to Alaska, which has always been my bucket list vacation! Our son Jeremy is doing well in a job I hope he loves. He got married about two years ago to a wonderful young woman, Joy. They recently had their first child, Olivia. How truly blessed we are! Needless to say, John and I are ecstatic that we are grandparents!

I guess my point is, we have all successfully found our own way to continue our lives without Joey. It is possible to be happy, even after such a traumatic loss. It does get better. It's just different. But I will not kid you. It is not easy, and you have to work hard at it! I still have my good and bad days, and probably always will. There are days that feel like Joey just died, and I'm a big mess! Yet I know that this is normal and will pass. On those difficult days, especially, I try to concentrate on how truly blessed I and my family still are. And although we only had Joey in our lives for a short twenty years, we were able to enjoy him and make wonderful memories with him that will last our lifetimes.

Additionally, when Joey died, my whole perspective of life changed, and so did my priorities. After such a major loss, you truly do realize what is important in life. I spend as much time as I can with those I love, my immediate close family and friends. And I cherish and strive to enjoy every moment I am fortunate to share with them. I also appreciate the little things in life, even if that sounds corny. I notice the beautiful blue skies, the fluffy white clouds and appreciate them and the beauty of nature. I love sparkles on my clothes, my shoes and anything else. They make me happy and I don't apologize for that.

I have found that keeping busy and always having something, even small, to look forward to, like sleeping in on a Sunday morning, or having lunch with a friend, helps me. I try to stay positive and see the good in people and situations. I truly believe in gratitude. I thank God every night for the good things that happened that day, and every morning for the privilege of having another day. I am trying to live my life this way.

I was raised Catholic, and before Joey died, if anyone asked me did I have faith, I answered absolutely. But I really didn't. Now I have faith. I continue to believe that even when we die, our souls, our essence lives on. I believe there is something after death, be it heaven or something else. I now believe that reincarnation is a possibility. I do believe Joey's soul lives on, and I strongly feel that some of my experiences I shared with you prove this for me. I still watch for signs I feel he sends us, and I do feel his presence with me often. But I realize these are my beliefs and of course not everyone shares them. And that is okay. We all have the right to believe what we want and I respect that. I always say, I may die and find out I was wrong and there is nothing, but if what I believe gets me through the day, I'm good with that! So until that day when I believe I will be reunited with Joey and all my loved ones on the other side, I will continue to live the best life I can.

Endnotes:

Chapter 9
[1] The television series "Knight Rider" originally broadcast on NBC from 1982 to 1985.

Chapter 12
[2] Betty Boop is an animated cartoon character created by Max Fleischer, with help from animators including Grim Natwick. She originally appeared in the Talkartoon and Betty Boop film series, which were produced by Fleischer Studios and released by Paramount Pictures.

Chapter 15
[3] Pearl Jam is an American rock band formed in 1990 in Seattle, Washington. Since its inception, the band's line-up has included Eddie Vedder, Mike McCready, Stone Gossard and Jeff Ament. Since 1998, the band has also included drummer Matt Cameron.

Chapter 16
[4] Stephen Ray Vaughn was an American musician, singer, songwriter and record producer, and one of the most influential guitarists in the revival of blues in the 1980s.

[5] Wheel of Fortune slot machines stem from one of the most popular game shows "Wheel of Fortune." The show's music, sound effects, and the wheel itself have become unmistakable in American culture. It's these features of the show that create the basis for the Wheel of Fortune slot machines by IGT.

Chapter 18
[6] "On Death and Dying," a book by Elisabeth Kubler Ross.

Chapter 23
[7] The 1999 film, "The Sixth Sense," tells the story of Cole Sear (played by Haley Joel Osment), a troubled, isolated boy who is able to see and talk to the dead, and an equally troubled child psychologist named Malcolm Crowe (played by Bruce Willis) who tries to help him.

Chapter 26
[8] "The Blair Witch Project" is a1999 horror film. Three film students vanish after traveling into a Maryland forest to film a documentary on the local Blair Witch legend, leaving only their footage behind.

Chapter 32
[9] "With Arms Wide Open" was a song from the album "Human Clay," the second studio album by the American rock band Creed released on September 28, 1999 through Wind-up Records.

[10] Lee Jun-fan known professionally as Bruce Lee, was a Hong Kong and American actor, film director, martial artist, martial arts instructor, philosopher, and founder of the martial art Jeet Kune Do, one of the wushu or Kungfu styles.

Chapter 37
[11] The television program "What Would You Do" originally broadcast on ABC on February 26, 2008. It is presented by John Quiñones and is currently in its thirteenth season.

Chapter 38
[12] A Tupperware party is run by a Tupperware "consultant" for a host who invites friends and neighbors into his or her home to see the product line. Tupperware hosts are rewarded with free products based on the level of sales made at their party.